50
Reproducible
Strategy Sheets

That Build Comprehension During Independent Reading

Engaging Forms That Guide Students to Use Reading
Strategies and Recognize Literary Elements—
And Help You Assess Comprehension

By Anina Robb

SCHOLASTIC
PROFESSIONAL BOOKS

New York • Toronto • London • Auckland • Sydney • Mexico City
New Delhi • Hong Kong • Buenos Aires

DEDICATION:

For my dear husband, Rob,
who encourages me to pursue my dreams.

Cover design by Josue Castilleja
Interior design by Holly Grundon

ISBN: 0-439-38784-1
Copyright © 2003 by Anina Robb
All rights reserved. Published by Scholastic Inc.
Printed in the U.S.A.

8 9 10   40   09 08 07 06 05 04

Contents

Introduction 5

The Benefits of Independent Reading 6

Making Independent Reading Work in Your Classroom 6

How to Use This Book 8

Making the Most of Independent Reading 9

Part 1: *Record-Keeping Forms*

Record-Keeping Forms 13

    My Reading Agreement: A Contract 14

    My Reading Log: A Record 15

Part 2: *Before-Reading Strategies*

Before-Reading Strategies 16

    Title and Cover Web: Activate Prior Knowledge 18

    Fast Write: Make Connections to Text 19

    Picture Walk: Preview-Analyze-Predict-Connect (Informational Picture Books) . . . 20

    Picture Walk: Preview-Analyze-Predict-Connect (Fiction Picture Books) 22

Part 3: *During- and After-Reading Strategies*

Strategies That Work With Any Genre 24

    What's Next?: Predict-Support-Adjust 27

    Pleased to Meet You: Draw Conclusions About a Character 28

    Making My Own Movie: Visualize 29

    Important Scenes: Visualize Setting 31

    Be a Reporter: Retell 32

    Stay Curious!: Question 33

    Stay Connected: Make Personal Connections 35

    Storyboard Sequence: Track the Main Events 36

    Seeing the Difference: Compare and Contrast 38

Strategies for Reading Nonfiction 39

    What Do I Want to Know?: KWL 42

    Zoom In on Key Details: Identify Details—The 5 W's 43

    Understanding Relationships: Determine Cause and Effect 44

    Seeing the Big Picture: Identify Main Idea and Key Details 45

    Thinking Links: Make Connections to the World 46

Strategies for Reading Poetry 47

    Become a Telescope: Complete a Close Reading of a Poem 49

Word Links: Explore Connotation and Denotation 50
Say It Your Way: Paraphrase 51
Savor Your Senses: Identify Sensory Images 52

Part 4: *Helping Students Understand Literary Elements*

Exploring Fiction 53
Who Is It?: Character Mapping 57
Climb the Mountain: Examine Plot Structure 59
What's the Problem?: Identify Problem and Outcome 60
The Big Picture: Explore Genre: Realistic Fiction 61
Step Back in Time: Explore Genre: Historical Fiction 62
Imaginary Worlds: Explore Genre: Fantasy 63

Exploring Folk and Fairy Tales 65
Tasks That Test: Explore Genre: Folk and Fairy Tales 66
What Makes It a Tale?: Explore Genre: Folk and Fairy Tales 67

Exploring Poetry 69
Dig Those Natural Rhythms: Explore Rhythm 72
Give It a Break!: Identify Stanzas 73
Rock and Rhyme: Determine Rhyme 74
Seeing With Simile: Find Similes 75
Memorable Metaphors: Find Metaphors 76
Smooth Sounds: Use Alliteration 77
Oh! The Sounds You'll Hear!: Identify Onomatopoeia 78

Exploring Biography and Autobiography 79
Making a Difference: Note Key Accomplishments 80
Life's Building Blocks: Determine Important Influences 81
How Am I Like You?: Make Connections 82
How They Helped the World: Synthesize Information 83

Exploring Informational Books 84
Seeking Solutions: Identify Problem-Solution Text Structure 86
Do the Facts Add Up?: Distinguish Fact and Opinion 87
Questioning the Reader: Ask Questions 88
Once Upon a Time . . . : Make Personal Connections 89

Part 5: *Strategies to Help Students With Word Study*

Strategies to Help Students With Word Study 90
Word Detectives: Use Context Clues 92
Questioning the Word: Create a Vocabulary Web 93
Context to Connection: Perform a Word Study 94
Take Apart a Word: Perform a Word Study 95

Notes 96

Introduction

"I can't read this book, Ms. Robb." Alberto strode up to my side and gazed at me from under his long eyelashes.

"Why not?" I asked.

"What kind of name is Sadako? This book doesn't have anything to do with me."

I thought for a moment: Alberto was in the 4th grade. He was Dominican and had never been out of the Bronx. Japan might as well have been the moon to Alberto. But I suggested this book because I thought Alberto could connect to the feeling of hope in the story. I knew that he had suffered many losses like Sadako. But I also knew he came to school each day eager and smiling.

"Give it a try, Alberto," I nudged. "It's about this girl who loves to run."

He interrupted, "I am the fastest boy in this class." I smiled and continued.

"She's got a terrible problem, though, and . . ." Alberto looked at the book.

"I'll try it." He started back to his desk, reading while he walked.

Alberto hesitated when confronted with reading *Sadako and the Thousand Paper Cranes*. He didn't think he'd be able to connect to the story. He thought it would be of no interest to him. Because I knew a little bit about Alberto, I guessed he would really love the book and that he would connect to Sadako's love of running and her fearlessness, which he shared. Alberto read and reread *Sadako and the Thousand Paper Cranes* four times that year. Each time he was surprised by something new.

I've had many students like Alberto initially reject a book that I've suggested for their independent reading. By listening to students' fears and concerns about a book and giving them a way into the book—for instance, with a short anecdote from the story or information about the author—I can usually tempt them to try it. Designating class time for this independent reading further encourages them, and I've found that incorporating independent reading into my daily schedule has enriched my students' learning—and fostered a love of reading.

The Benefits of Independent Reading

Independent reading allows me to teach reading to a heterogeneous class of students at many different levels. Once everyone is settled with a book they can read—gaining valuable reading practice, building background knowledge in areas that interest them—I am suddenly free to confer with individual students, providing just the scaffolding that each one needs to move ahead as a reader. Children who had written, "I hate reading," on their reading surveys now protest when the lights flash, signaling the end of independent reading. In an independent reading program, all students—from below grade-level readers to proficient ones—have a chance to succeed, monitor their improvements, and challenge themselves.

What Research Says About Independent Reading

In addition to my own classroom experience, the research solidly indicates that independent reading helps all readers improve their skills. Here's a sampling of recent research findings:

- According to Fielding and Pearson (*Educational Leadership*, 51 (5) 1994), dependent readers, grade-level readers, and proficient readers all benefit from independent reading.

- Richard Allington (*Elementary School Journal*, 83, 1983) showed that dependent readers, when given chunks of time to read during the school day, make more progress by reading literature than from completing skills worksheets.

- the best way to improve reading is to read, read, read!

Making Independent Reading Work in Your Classroom

A classroom grounded in independent reading succeeds because it engages every child in the room. Here are some things that I do in my classroom to facilitate independent reading:

- **Offer students choices** in the books they read. Let them select from several books at their independent or easy reading levels.

- **Help students find books that interest them.** At the beginning of the year, I survey my students about their reading interests so I can point them toward books they might enjoy. I also divide my classroom library into "genre shelves," so that students who are fascinated by fantasy, for example, can zoom in on the fantasy and science fiction shelves.

- **Read aloud several times a day.** This shows your students how important reading is to you. Read-aloud time will quickly become a "sacred" time in your class that neither you nor your students want to skip.

- **Share some personal stories about your reading life** with the students. Tell them about a great book, magazine, or newspaper article that you've read.

- **Reserve 20-30 minutes a day for independent reading.** When you make time for independent reading, your students understand how important it is. If I am not conferencing with a student during this time, I will often read a book, too.

- **Encourage students to find a comfortable space when they read.** Under a desk, on a pillow, and leaning against a wall are some favorite reading places in my classroom.

- **Set aside time for students to talk about a favorite book with classmates.** This will inspire other children to read. In my classroom, students write "Thumbs-Up!" reviews on index cards. I post these brief book reviews on a bulletin board. Students check out what their classmates have read and liked, and these reviews often prompt students to try a book they might otherwise have overlooked.

Every class has its own personality, range of ability, and pace. I'm sure that you will find, as I have, that independent reading is a great way to turn students into active, motivated participants in their own learning. The strategy sheets in this book are the tools my students and I use to make the most of independent reading.

How to Use This Book

I have put together in this book ideas and materials that will help you explore ways to motivate your students to become independent, thoughtful readers. These strategy sheets will guide your independent reading instruction in three ways:

1. By focusing on strengthening the reading skills students need to develop as readers. While using the strategies, your students will pause and think about what they read; they will begin to monitor what they understand and consider what they are learning.

2. By providing you with a way to assess each student's reading abilities.

3. By serving as a built-in structure for you to manage an independent reading program in your classroom.

In doing so, the strategies and graphic organizers in this book are tools to help you guide students to become active participants in reading and learning.

I've organized this book into five sections. The strategy sheets in parts I and II can be used with any genre. Those in part III emphasize the application of reading strategies to different genres in order to deepen students' comprehension and to enlarge their vocabulary and background knowledge. The goal of the sheets in Part IV is to build students' knowledge of the various literary elements of a wide range of genres. Finally, the sheets in part V focuses on word study and can be used with any genre. By understanding different genre structures, students gain the knowledge needed to experiment with a genre in their own writing. Throughout the book, the strategy sheets invite students to respond thoughtfully to literature, and you can then use their responses as springboards for mini-lessons in writing workshop.

It is not necessary to have students complete every single worksheet. View this book as a comprehensive menu from which you can pick and choose the items that will nourish and meet your students' unique needs. The following sections of this introduction present ideas you can use to set the tone for a productive, focused independent reading program. There is also discussion on how to use the strategy sheets in this book to support your independent reading program.

Why Do You Read?

To help your students become aware of the various purposes for reading, begin a discussion by asking, "Why do you read?" "How does it make you feel?" Then share any of the following ideas with your students.

ENJOYMENT - Reading is a great way to entertain yourself.

EASE - Reading happens automatically every day. You read signs, headlines, and food labels.

MEANING - Reading teaches you new facts and new ideas.

INFORMATION - Reading helps you understand the world around you. You can learn about current events and computers. You can learn how to play the piano or make a cake.

APPRECIATION - Reading a well-crafted poem, story, novel, letter, or article can develop an appreciation of the writer's craft and teach you to read like a writer.

Refer to this discussion often and encourage students to consider their own purposes for reading specific pieces.

Making the Most of Independent Reading

Setting a Purpose

Setting a purpose for reading is a sure way to guide students to become active, engaged readers. Model for your students, by thinking aloud, how readers consider the purpose before reading. Tell them there are many different purposes for reading: sometimes people read to answer questions or wonderings, or to relate to a person, event, or emotion; other times people read to clarify information or to enjoy language and story. Always encourage your students to preview a text and think about why they are reading before they dive in; this process builds motivation to read and enhances comprehension, since students are actively reading with a purpose in mind.

Choosing the Book

When I walk into the local library and see all of the novels lining the shelves that run up and down the entire first floor, I get a little overwhelmed. How do I know which book to choose?

The first thing I consider is my purpose for reading. Is it enjoyment? Well, then a mystery novel or a romance might do. Or, do I want to reread a book that I didn't really get into the first time or that I did not understand and therefore ought to read again to clarify things? Or do I, perhaps, need to find a book that will provide information on a specific topic?

After I've decided upon my purpose for reading, I can narrow my selection. The key to success for all readers is to select books that they want to read and that they are comfortable reading. This way, readers — and in this case, students — will develop fluency, expand their vocabulary, and most of all, enjoy reading.

The Just-Right Book

The five-finger method is an easy tool students can use to decide if a book is "just right" for them. Ask each student to turn to any page in the book he or she has chosen. If there are more than five words on the page that the student cannot pronounce or doesn't understand, the book is too hard. Suggest that the student save this book for another time. Or, if it's appropriate, you might offer to read it aloud to the class. You can also partner up students as they select books. Having a partner ensures that the students will monitor each other as they choose a "just-right" book.

Demonstrate the five-finger method to your class by thinking aloud and explaining that some books are even too hard for you to read! Use authentic examples: I often bring in my husband's technical computer books as an example of reading that is neither at my level nor in my interest range. Stress that independent reading should be pleasant and not a chore.

Choosing the Right Book

"Yesterday I was in the library. I was looking for a book to give me some information on fixing a leaky sink. I found a section of books intended just for plumbers. When I opened one to the first page, there were so many words and terms that I couldn't understand, I became frustrated. The book was too difficult to be helpful to me. I put the book down and chose another one that was for 'do-it-yourself' fixer-uppers. Everything in that book was clearly explained, and there were great pictures that illustrated the directions. I knew that was the right book for me."

Tips for Using the Strategy Worksheets to Manage Independent Reading

Modeling to Support Students

The time you take to show students how you might complete a form is extremely valuable to them. Why? Because students can observe and listen to your expectations, then complete their work following your demonstration guidelines.

◎ Read the entire form first to assess what you need to do. Think aloud to show students the directions that you understand and those you need to reread to clarify.

◎ Demonstrate, on chart paper or on an overhead transparency, how you go about answering each section. Think aloud to let students in on your mental process, then write down your thoughts.

◎ Reserve a few minutes after you model each section and invite students to pose questions. Respond to their questions.

◎ Model how you go back and check that your answers are written clearly and that you've completed the entire form.

Moving Students to Independence

Once you've modeled using a particular strategy sheet, invite students to try it on their own. The first few times, it's helpful to review the sheet, discussing the strategy and reminding students to preview the text and set a purpose for reading. As students become more confident with a strategy, you can pair them with others who may need more support. Once students are successful with a form, you can move them to using the form independently with a variety of reading materials.

Assessment

Once students grasp a particular strategy, you can ask them to complete the worksheet for that strategy and evaluate their work. Make sure, however, that students can experience success. You should probably have them complete two to four of the same or similar forms before setting them to work for a grade. Here are some things to look for when you read students' work:

- **Work is very general.** If a student's work lacks specific details, you might want to check to see if the book is too challenging. If the book is a good match to a student's reading level, sit side-by-side with the student and scaffold or support learning by helping him or her find specific details from the reading material.

- **Work has blank sections.** First, ask the student why he or she did not complete a section. It might be an oversight, or it could be that the student did not understand the directions. Avoid punishing students by taking off points. Instead, help students understand what they need to do, then give them time to complete the work.

- **Writing is unclear.** Have students read what they wrote out loud. Next, ask them to add more details and reformulate their ideas orally. When they can explain their ideas orally, they can write them on the worksheet. You might have to model what a clear response sounds like before asking them to redo their unclear answers.

Now that you have an idea of what this book is about — how the strategies can aid you in helping your students become better, more engaged readers, and how to incorporate the sheets into your independent reading program — it's time to start putting it all to work.

PART 1

Record-Keeping Forms

The following two forms, a reading contract and a reading log, provide an easy, manageable way to engage students in the reading process from the beginning. These reproducible worksheets focus on developing reading independence for students while facilitating management and record keeping for teachers. They encourage students to develop their own reading tastes and become lifelong readers. Students also learn to pace themselves and take responsibility for their own learning.

My Reading Agreement: A Contract

The reading contract is the place where students set their goals for reading. Generally, I find it beneficial to use the first school day of each month as a goal-setting day. Have students commit, in writing, to the number of books they will read that month. (A struggling reader may only aim to complete one book or several easy-to-read books he or she can complete quickly and comprehend.) File the contracts in individual student folders so students can pull their file and monitor their progress.

My Reading Log: A Record

The reading log is a place where students record what they have read, and it's a great way for students to take personal responsibility for their learning and to chart their progress. Set aside a few minutes of class time once or twice a week for students to log in their books. Encourage students to enter a new title soon after it has been read, and ask them to rate each book by checking the appropriate spot on the form. File completed logs with students' reading contracts. Students will be proud and amazed in June when they see all the books they have read!

Name: _____ Date: _____

My Reading Agreement: A Contract

DIRECTIONS: Think about how many books you want to read this month. Fill in and sign the agreement. Tell your teacher at least 3 days before the end of the month if you feel you cannot complete your reading. Together, agree on a new number and due date.

My goal is to read _____ books

during the month of _____ .

If I can't meet my agreement I will speak to my teacher at least three days before the end of the month to make an adjustment.

Student's name _____

Teacher's name _____

Name: _____

Date: _____

My Reading Log: A Record

DIRECTIONS: Record the title, author, and the date you begin and end each book in the log. When you finish the book, rate the book: thumbs up, okay, or thumbs down.

How This Helps

Keeping track of what you've read is a great way to take charge of your learning. Plus, you will have a record of all the great books you've read this year.

Title	Author	Date Started	Date Finished	Rating
				☐ Thumbs Up ☐ Okay ☐ Thumbs Down
				☐ Thumbs Up ☐ Okay ☐ Thumbs Down
				☐ Thumbs Up ☐ Okay ☐ Thumbs Down
				☐ Thumbs Up ☐ Okay ☐ Thumbs Down

50 Reproducible Strategy Sheets That Build Comprehension During Independent Reading   Scholastic Professional Books

Before-Reading Strategies

The three forms in this section provide an easy, manageable way to get students ready for their reading. They encourage students to think before diving into a book. Calling upon prior knowledge and connecting to the text before reading will warm students up to topics and improve their comprehension.

Title and Cover Web: Activate Prior Knowledge

A title and cover web is a brainstorming strategy that activates students' prior knowledge and connects them to the text. Use this strategy before reading. In my experience, this exercise excites students about choosing a book; thinking before reading whets their appetite and motivates them to find out more.

Fast Write: Make Connections to Text

"Fast writing" is writing without self-editing; it is concerned with ideas and connections, not with grammar, punctuation, spelling, or handwriting. Use this strategy before reading to get students thinking about what they already know about a topic. It is helpful to start with a time limit of two minutes of writing. Eventually, work students up to five minutes. Encourage students to make connections to their lives, other books, and movies. If time permits, have students discuss their fast writes with partners to discover other connections.

Here's an example of one student's fast write. Make photocopies or an overhead transparency to show your students how a "fast write" might look.

Sample Fast Write

This book, <u>Stone Fox</u>, looks like an adventure because of the cover picture of the boy running and the sled. It looks really cold and reminds me of winter which I am not happy about. I don't like being cold and sick although snow is nice. Stones are hard and dead and cold. I wonder what they have to do with a fox. I usually think of foxes as... I don't know. I don't know... sly and fast and being hunted.

Picture Walk: Preview-Analyze-Predict-Connect

This pair of worksheets — one for fiction and one for nonfiction — helps students collect ideas, words, and clues from illustrations or charts that can help them better understand the text. Instead of feeling only frustration when faced with new ideas, students will be prepared. This strategy guides students to think about the whole in terms of its parts by taking a "picture walk." On a picture walk, you invite the students to study the pictures in a selection to get a sense of the setting, characters, and plot. In the case of nonfiction, students get a preview of photographs, illustrations, charts, and other graphic elements. Introduce this strategy by modeling. Let students in on your thought processes and think aloud, showing them the way you make predictions and connections when you take a picture walk through a book.

Name: _____   Date: _____

Title and Cover Web

DIRECTIONS: Look at the cover illustration of your book. Read the title, back cover, and first page. Record the title in the center box below, then fill in the other boxes with all of your ideas.

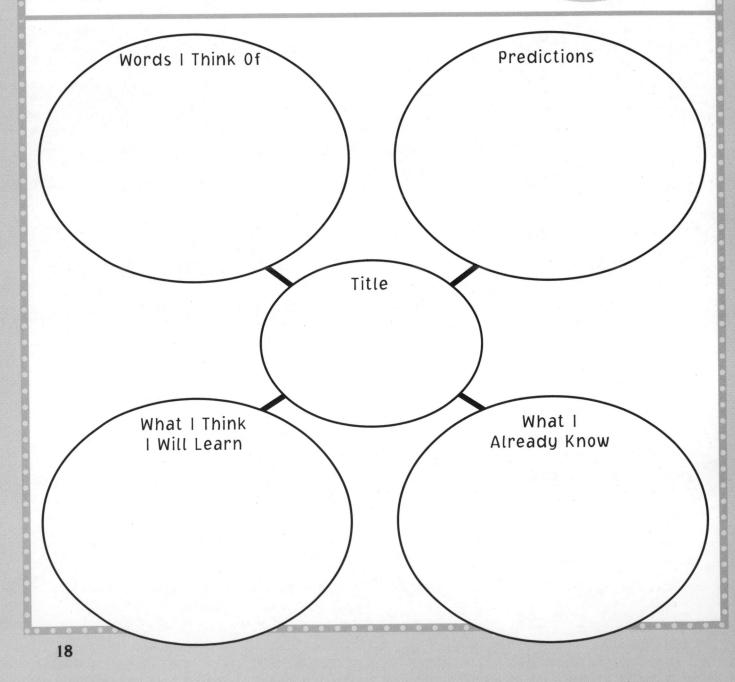

Words I Think Of

Predictions

Title

What I Think
I Will Learn

What I
Already Know

18

Name: _____   Date: _____

Fast Write

DIRECTIONS: Look at the cover of your book. Read the title, back cover, and first page. Then start writing all of the ideas that come into your head. Don't worry about sentences, spelling, or grammar, just keep writing until time is called. You can repeat words or write "I don't know" until you get a fresh idea. Continue writing on the back if you run out of space.

How This Helps

A fast write opens up your mind so you can make connections and find information or ideas that you didn't even realize you knew.

IDEA BOX

Try connecting the book to:

Your life

What you know about this book

Other books you've read

Questions about the book

Set a Purpose

Think about why you want to read this story.
Write about it on the back of this page.

Name: _____ Date: _____

Picture Walk (Informational Picture Books)

DIRECTIONS:

1. Read the title of your book and look at the cover.

2. Take a picture walk through the book.

3. Read the back cover.

4. Read the first page.

5. Write what you learned form your preview and make predictions and connections in the spaces below.

How This Helps

Thinking before you read helps you connect to the story or the new ideas.

PREVIEW

List 5 things you learned from the preview:

1. _____

2. _____

3. _____

4. _____

5. _____

PREDICT

Now, write a prediction: I think this book will be about _____

_____

_____

_____

50 Reproducible Strategy Sheets That Build Comprehension During Independent Reading   Scholastic Professional Books

because

CONNECT

Connect what you think this book will be about to your own life.

IDEA BOX

Connect to:
Friends
Movies
Magazines
Family
Other books

Set a Purpose

Think about why you want to read this book. Write about it here.

Name: _____ Date: _____

Picture Walk (Fiction Picture Books)

1. Read the title, front, and back cover.
2. Read the chapter titles if the book has these. Look at any illustrations.
3. Read the first chapter.
4. Complete the preview chart and make your predictions and connections on the next page.

How This Helps

Thinking before you read helps you connect to the story or the new ideas.

Preview Chart of First Chapter

Characters	Setting	Conflict
List the characters and what you learned about them.	Describe the setting.	Write any problems.

50 Reproducible Strategy Sheets That Build Comprehension During Independent Reading Scholastic Professional Books

PREDICT

What do you think this book will be about?

I think this story will be about _____

_____

_____

_____

_____

CONNECT

Connect what you think this story will be about to your own life.

_____

_____

_____

_____

_____

IDEA BOX

Connect to:
Friends
Movies
Magazines
Family
Other books

Set a Purpose

Think about why you want to read this story. Write about it here.

_____

_____

PART 3

During- and After- Reading Strategies

Strategies That Work With Any Genre

Good readers use strategies to construct meaning and to monitor what they understand and what confuses them. The seven strategies in this section will help you teach students to interact with the text by predicting, questioning, retelling, drawing conclusions, making connections, and visualizing.

What's Next?: Predict-Support-Adjust

When you ask your students to make a prediction, you are asking them to use both what they know about the text and their prior knowledge to figure out what will happen next in the story or what a character will do. Explain to students that when they make predictions, they are detectives, using many clues. They can use the title, illustrations, and the text as evidence to support their predictions. High-level thinking occurs when students find support in the text for their predictions because they must choose explicit and inferred details. After reading, ask students to adjust their predictions based on whether or not what they thought matches the text. Adjusting predictions after reading gives students time to reflect on what they learned and evaluate their prediction.

Pleased to Meet You:
Draw Conclusions About Character

Drawing conclusions is a critical thinking activity related to making inferences. In this activity, ask students to think about a person or character from their reading. To draw a conclusion about the character that is not stated in the text, the students can study the following elements: dialogue; a character's inner thoughts; a character's actions, decisions, relationship with others; what others say about the character; and how a character acts in a specific setting. Model for your students how you would draw a conclusion about a character from a text you've all read based on each of these elements. When reading historical fiction, biography, or autobiography, you can draw conclusions about a person's decisions, actions, or interactions.

Making My Own Movie: Visualize

Engage your students by telling them that good readers visualize, or make movies in their heads: the mind is a screen and the text projects images of various elements, such as what a character and a setting look like. Research shows that you visualize what you truly understand. So when a student can visualize elements of the text, you know that he or she has a deep understanding of its content.

Important Scenes: Visualize Setting

Excite students by asking them, "How might your life change if you lived in the desert (or a swamp, or on a tundra)?" "What problems might this setting cause?" "How might the setting help you?" Remind students that both fiction and non-fiction writing contain settings, and that the settings affect both the people in the stories and the plot (or events) of the story or the person's life. Encourage students to keep a close eye out for details about the story's time and place, including sensory details. Understanding how a setting works in a story helps students understand both the characters and the plot.

Be a Reporter: Retell

Encourage your students to retell the story when they come to the end of a chapter or to retell their favorite part of a story. Students can also summarize/retell an article or section of a nonfiction text. Measuring their ability to retell what they've read is a good way to assess students' comprehension and recall. In your students' retellings, look for sequencing of events, names of people or characters, setting, problems, and rich details.

Stay Curious: Question

This strategy can be used before, during, and after reading. Before reading, questioning gets students ready to read by involving them in the story. When students raise questions during reading, they are monitoring what they understand, what confuses them, and what they wonder about plot, conflicts, and characters. After reading, students can pose their own questions for discussion. Explain to students the difference between factual and open-ended questions: factual questions have one answer, while open-ended questions can have two or more answers or responses.

Stay Connected: Make Personal Connections

Personal connections give relevance to the text and help students see a reason for reading. Connecting to a text can move students beyond their own experience and connect them to other people's lives and world issues, such as caring for the environment, poverty, and having compassion for different kinds of people. Students can connect to a character's problems, the setting, events, conflicts, and information.

Storyboard Sequence: Track the Main Events

A storyboard is a visual and written way to keep track of a story's major events and the order in which they happened. Ask students to be selective and choose only the main scenes when they create their storyboard. This strategy not only enhances reading but can also be used by students to plan their own writing. Moreover, it is a great introduction to summary writing, as students must focus on the essential details.

Seeing the Difference: Compare and Contrast

Spark students' interest in comparing and contrasting by asking them if they ever compare movies and books, different athletes, or music groups. Lead them to understand that readers can make comparisons about different literary elements like character, plot, or setting, in a story or about historical figures or events in nonfiction. Comparing and contrasting elements of a text not only helps students find and organize details, but it engages them in analyzing similarities and differences. This close examination of the elements gives the text relevance as students understand how these elements work together or individually. I've found students enjoy extending this activity after they have read a number of selections, comparing and contrasting across texts and not just within them.

Name: _____ Date: _____

What's Next?

DIRECTIONS: Read the title, back cover, and first page of your book. Look at the cover illustration. Think about what you already know about books and the clues that you have just uncovered.

1. Predict what you think this story will be about.

2. Support your prediction with evidence from the title, cover, and first page.

3. After reading, adjust your prediction so it matches the text.

How This Helps

Thinking about a book before you read helps you discover what you already know so you can connect to the book.

1. **My Prediction:** I think this story will be about _____

_____

_____

2. **My Support:** I made this prediction because _____

_____

Set a Purpose

Use your prediction to set a purpose for reading. Write it here.

_____

3. **My Adjustment:** After reading the book, I see that my prediction

(matches/does not match) the text because _____

_____

_____

50 Reproducible Strategy Sheets That Build Comprehension During Independent Reading   Scholastic Professional Books

Name: _____   Date: _____

Pleased to Meet You

DIRECTIONS: Choose a character from the story and fill in the organizer below. Then use the information you've recorded to draw a conclusion about the character.

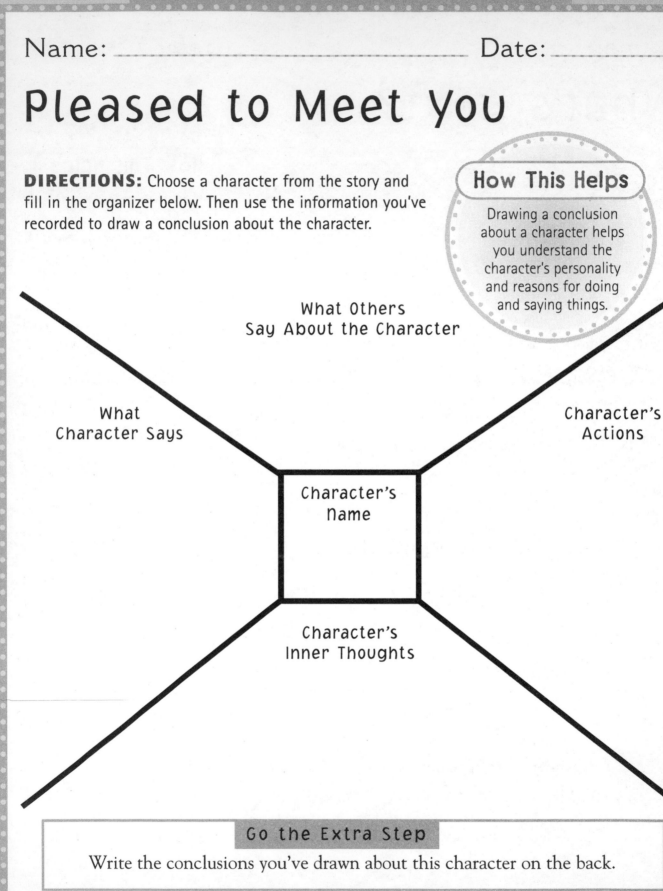

What Others
Say About the Character

What
Character Says

Character's
Actions

Character's
Name

Character's
Inner Thoughts

Go the Extra Step

Write the conclusions you've drawn about this character on the back.

50 Reproducible Strategy Sheets That Build Comprehension During Independent Reading   Scholastic Professional Books

Name: _____ Date: _____

Making My Own Movie

DIRECTIONS:

1. Preview the book by reading the title and looking at the cover. Imagine what the story will be about and try to picture the characters and settings in your mind. Write about your predictions below. Then read the story or book.

2. Picture in your mind a character in the book at the beginning and at the end. Then draw the character at each time in the spaces on the next page. Explain how the character changes.

How This Helps

Visualizing helps you "see" what you understand in a story.

Set a Purpose

What images do you expect to see in your mind as you read this story? Write about them here.

_____

_____

_____

_____

_____

_____

_____

Visualize It!

Write About It

Draw the Character
at the **Beginning** of the story.

Explain why the character looks this way to you. Think of what happened to gather clues.

_____

_____

_____

List words that tell what he/she is like.

_____

_____

_____

Draw the Character
at the **End** of the story.

Describe how the character changed.

_____

_____

_____

List words that tell what he/she is like now.

_____

_____

_____

Name: _____   Date: _____

Important Scenes

DIRECTIONS:

1. Read the story or article and ask, "Which settings greatly affect the main character?"

2. After reading, imagine how this important setting would look in your mind. Then sketch it. Hint: Include details that show time and the five senses (see, hear, smell, taste, touch).

3. Then, explain how the setting changes, helps, or creates problems for the main character.

How This Helps

Understanding the setting helps you understand the characters and the plot of a story.

Visualize It!

Write About It

_____

_____

_____

_____

_____

_____

Connect to Character: _____

_____

_____

Name: _____ Date: _____

Be a Reporter

DIRECTIONS: Read a chapter or two to three pages in your book or article. Think about the important information that you learned. Focus on the events, the characters/people, the setting, and the problem. Write what you remember in your own words below.

How This Helps

Retelling helps you understand and remember what happens in a story. It also helps you learn new information because the retelling is in your own words.

Chapter Title or Page Number(s) _____

My Retelling: _____

_____

_____

_____

_____

_____

_____

_____

_____

Name: _____ Date: _____

Stay Curious!

DIRECTIONS:

1. Before you read, complete the first three items below, telling what you know about the topic, any questions you have, and your purpose for this reading.

2. As you read, ask yourself, "Is this making sense?" Try to understand the story by rereading. Then retell or put the confusing parts in your own words in the "During Reading" space below.

3. When you finish, answer the questions in the "After Reading" box.

How This Helps

When you read, it is important to be aware of what you do and don't understand.

Before You Read

1. What do I know about the topic? _____

_____

_____

2. What questions do I have? _____

_____

_____

_____

Set a Purpose

Think about what you would like to learn from this story. Write about it here.

_____

_____

During Reading

In your own words, retell a confusing part or describe something new you learned.

_____

_____

_____

_____

_____

After Reading

1. What questions do I still have? _____

_____

_____

2. Ask a factual question (with only one answer).

_____

_____

3. Ask an open-ended question (with two or more answers/responses).

_____

_____

_____

_____

Name: _____   Date: _____

Stay Connected

DIRECTIONS:

1. Read the story and ask, "How can I link the reading to my life?"

2. After reading, see how many personal connections you can make. Fill in the chart with your ideas.

How This Helps

You will remember and understand more about what you read if you make a connection to it.

Connections I Made	What I Learned From My Connections
To the main character:	
To other characters:	
To the problem:	
To the setting:	
To events or conflicts:	

Name: _____   Date: _____

Storyboard Sequence

DIRECTIONS:

1. Read the story.

2. After reading, sketch what happens first. Write a note telling about your drawing.

3. Keep adding sketches and notes until you have included all of the MAIN events.

4. Retell the story to a partner, using your sketches to help you sequence the events.

How This Helps

A storyboard can help you keep track of the main events in a story and remember the order in which things happened.

1. Note: _____

_____

_____

_____

2. Note: _____

_____

_____

_____

3. Note: _____

_____

_____

4. Note: _____

_____

_____

5. Note: _____

_____

_____

6. Note: _____

_____

_____

Name: _____ Date: _____

Seeing the Difference

DIRECTIONS:

1. As you read, underline two events, settings, or people from your reading. Think about ways they are alike and different.

2. After reading, record what you learned about the events, settings, or people in the Venn diagram below. On the left-hand side, write the name of one event, person, or setting. Write the name of the second one on the right-hand side. Under each name, list all the differences. Where the circles overlap, list how these two things are similar.

Title and Author _____

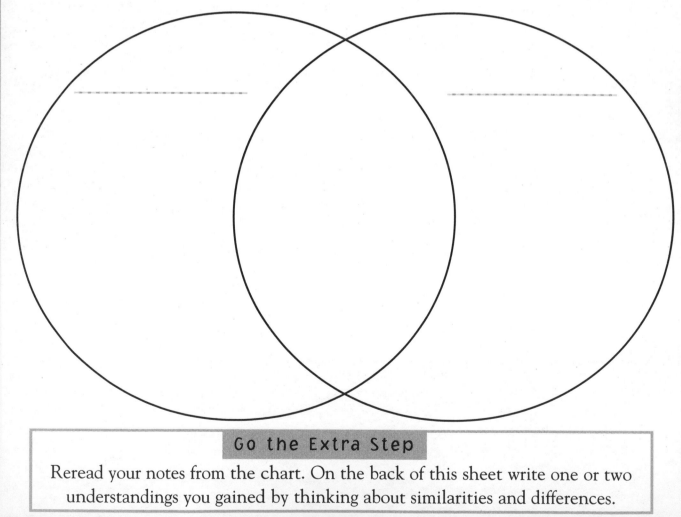

Go the Extra Step

Reread your notes from the chart. On the back of this sheet write one or two understandings you gained by thinking about similarities and differences.

Strategies for Reading Nonfiction

By the time students reach the fourth grade, they have a strong sense of the structure of stories. Now is a good time to emphasize reading nonfiction. Reading nonfiction expands students' background knowledge and deepens their understanding of the physical and natural world. Additionally, more and more standardized tests focus on nonfiction selections. The strategies in the following section will help you guide students to comprehend how nonfiction texts work and how to approach them in order to construct new understandings.

What Do I Want to Know?: KWL

A KWL chart is a great place for you to start with your students before they read new nonfiction. This strategy guides students to draw on what they already know about a subject and encourages them to make connections to their own experiences. Because it allows students to focus on what they want to learn, the KWL motivates them to read. Finally, after reading, it gives students a place to reflect on what they have learned.

Zoom In on Key Details: Identify Details—the 5 W's

The 5 W's graphic organizer provides a space for students to collect key information about the who, what, where, when, and why of a piece. Students can use this worksheet during reading as a note-taking tool or after reading to gather their thoughts and check their comprehension. It's also an easy way to connect reading and writing; students can use this exercise to brainstorm their own ideas about who, what, where, when, and why before writing their own pieces. Using this tool will help students make sure they include these five important nonfiction elements in their own writing.

Understanding Relationships: Determine Cause and Effect

The purpose of most nonfiction writing, including biography, autobiography, essays, newspaper stories, and textbook articles, is to explain why something happened. Consequently, nonfiction writers often use cause and effect to clarify the relationship between events. Before introducing this concept to your students, model an everyday example of cause and effect for them. Tell students that an event or situation happens that is *the cause*. This first event (cause) brings about a result that is *the effect.* Give them a few cause statements, such as: *My room is messy,* or *A foot of snow fell last night.* Brainstorm with students the many possible effects. Explain to students that understanding cause and effect is important because readers make connections to events when they think back on what they've read and see how causes have led to effects. Since this is sometimes a difficult concept for students to grasp, I suggest thinking aloud about a cause-and-effect relationship (see sample think aloud in the box below). And be sure to revisit the concept often so students have many opportunities to think and ask questions about it.

Think Aloud

Cause and Effect

"Usually actions or events that we call *causes* have consequences — or make something else happen, which we call an *effect.* Often a cause can have more than one effect. For example: Yesterday, I forgot to take the garbage out, so now the garbage cans are overflowing and I can't close the lids. There is a terrible smell coming from the cans, and we can't sit out in the back yard. And last night, a raccoon knocked over the cans because they were too full to close. So my first action — I didn't take out the garbage — is the cause. That first action, or cause, results in keeping me off my porch because it's messy and smelly. That's the effect."

Seeing the Big Picture: Identify Main Idea and Key Details

The main idea is the central or "big" idea in a piece of writing. It is the point the author wants you to remember. However, students often key into details first. Introduce the "big picture" strategy to your students when you think they are ready to sort out the big ideas and the smaller details. Encourage them to think about the details, then relate these to a big idea. You can also use this strategy as a springboard into a summary writing lesson: After reading, students should jot down the main idea; then have them create a list of four to five of the most important supporting details. Remind them that summaries are not long.

What's the main idea?

To help your students explore main idea, write these details on a chart and share them with the students:

◎   Feed Snuggles twice a day.

◎   Take Snuggles for a walk three times a day.

◎   Bathe Snuggles once a week.

◎   Play with Snuggles.

Here's a think aloud I present with the above chart:

"Can you figure out what the main idea is? These details all show what kind of care the dog named Snuggles needs. So the big idea is how to take care of Snuggles. Each detail shows one thing to do, like feed Snuggles or walk Snuggles. But notice that the main idea includes all of the details."

After the think aloud, ask students to explain how the detail statements are different from the main idea statement.

Thinking Links: Make Connections to the World

Helping your students connect to text makes reading more relevant to them. Explain that we read not only for entertainment but also to learn more about a subject or a topic. One way to do this is by making connections to our lives and the world. For instance, students could connect a character's situation to one a friend is going through, or they might relate an event to something going on in their school or town. The Idea Box on the worksheet has more suggestions on how students can connect to their reading. Impress upon students that the knowledge learned from reading can help them make good decisions in their own lives.

Name: _____   Date: _____

What Do I Want to Know?

DIRECTIONS:

1. Write the topic of your reading on the KWL chart below.

2. Before you read, write down what you already know about the topic in the "What I Know" column. Then write two to four questions you have about the topic in the "What I Want to Know" column.

3. Then set a purpose for reading; write it below.

4. After you read, fill in the "What I Learned Column."

Topic: _____

What I Know	What I Want to Know	What I Learned

Set a Purpose

Think about why you want to learn from this article. Write about it here.

_____

50 Reproducible Strategy Sheets That Build Comprehension During Independent Reading   Scholastic Professional Books

Name: _____ Date: _____

Zoom In on Key Details

DIRECTIONS:

1. Write the text's/article's subject on the subject line.
2. Preview the article, then read.
3. After you read, record key details about who, what, where, when, and why from the article.

How This Helps

The 5-W strategy helps you gather together important information about a topic by selecting the key details.

Subject: _____

Who	
What	
Where	
When	
Why	

Name: _____   Date: _____

Understanding Relationships

DIRECTIONS:

1. Read the book or article all the way through.

2. Underline or use sticky notes to mark a cause.

3. Think about how the cause changed or shaped things.

4. Write the cause in the "Cause" box; in the "Effect" box, write one or several effects that resulted from that cause.

5. Repeat for other causes in the text.

How This Helps

A cause-and-effect organizer helps show the relationships between events.

Remember, a CAUSE is the first event or situation. It results in another situation or event. That result is the EFFECT.

Cause	Effect
Example: I forgot to water my bean plant.	1. The leaves curled. 2. Some leaves fell off. 3. Others turned yellow.

Name: _____   Date: _____

Seeing the Big Picture

DIRECTIONS:

1. Read the book or article all the way through.

2. Write three important details below.

3. Think about the details and consider what the biggest, most important idea is. Write it at the bottom of the page.

How This Helps

Charting the main idea and the details helps you sort out the central, important ideas from the smaller details.

1. Detail _____

_____

2. Detail _____

_____

3. Detail _____

_____

IDEA BOX

What are the details? Check out:

Facts

Examples

Comments from experts (quotes)

Explanations

Descriptions

Sidebars

Main Idea: _____

_____

_____

_____

_____

Name: _____ Date: _____

Thinking Links

How This Helps

Making a Connections chart helps you link new information to your life, making the reading meaningful and more enjoyable.

DIRECTIONS:

1. Preview the article or book and set a purpose for reading.

2. Read the entire article or book.

3. After reading, write down what you learned and the connections you can make to the new information.

IDEA BOX

Connect to:

your life	friends/family
a movie	the community
other books	the world

What I learned	Connections I Made
1.	
2.	
3.	
4.	
5.	

Strategies for Reading Poetry

Reading poetry is a different experience from reading fiction and nonfiction. Poetry encourages us to look at words closely, to visualize, and to listen to the sounds of words. It's also a good place to start looking for meaning in writing. Because of the condensed form of a poem, many students are not afraid to jump right in. The four strategy sheets in this section invite your students to be active readers as they respond to poetry.

Become a Telescope: Complete a Close Reading of a Poem

Tell students that because poems are usually much shorter than works of prose, each word or line has been specifically chosen to deepen the poem's meaning. Doing a close reading of a poem helps readers appreciate the power of each word. Begin by reading a poem aloud several times. Encourage volunteers in the class to read the poem aloud so the poem can be heard in different voices. Once students have a feel for the poem, do a close reading, in which you think about each line, each word of the poem. Model for students how you focus on words or lines that catch your attention or that confuse you. Use the double-entry journal format—on chart paper or the overhead—to record your ideas and thoughts.

IDEA BOX

Encourage your students to read a poem many times. Remind them:

1. The first reading should be for pure enjoyment.

2. Look for clues to what the poem is saying during the second reading.

3. On the third reading, ask yourself, "How does the poem make me feel?"

4. Investigate the poem's structure on the fourth reading.

Word Links: Explore Connotation and Denotation

Denotation is the dictionary meaning of a word, while connotation is the emotional response that a word evokes. Knowing the connotation of a word enriches a poem. Help your students identify and consider connotations as they read and reread poetry. I like to give my students an example to illustrate: I point out that words that might mean the same but conjure up different feelings, like *tiptoeing* and *sneaking*. *Sneaking* seems much more negative and devious, while *tiptoeing* seems innocent.

Say It Your Way: Paraphrase

Use this strategy with your students to examine particular lines of a poem. These can be lines that the students liked or those they found surprising or difficult. Explain to students that when you paraphrase, you translate the author's words into your own. Impress upon students that the paraphrasing should be in their own words and in their own style.

Savor Your Senses: Identify Sensory Images

One of the fabulous things about reading poetry is the way it engages your five senses. Encourage students to become more aware of the images that pop into their heads as they read poems. Invite them to sketch any images that appeal to their senses: sight, hearing, taste, smell, and touch. Focusing on these sensual images helps students spotlight the specific language of the poem.

IDEA BOX

In Their Own Words

Students can paraphrase in a number of different learning situations. Have them practice this skill in these scenarios:

Class discussion

Conversations with a reading partner

Journal entries

Summary

An original poem modeled after the one they've read

Name: _____ Date: _____

Become a Telescope

DIRECTIONS:

1. Read the poem out loud and to yourself several times.

2. As you're rereading, notice words or lines that you like, catch your attention, or seem important. Write these on the left side of the double-entry journal.

3. On the right side, write what you think the words mean, how they make you feel, and what they lead you to think about.

4. When you're finished with the journal, read the poem through again. Write your thoughts or insights about the poem on the back of this sheet.

How This Helps

Close reading helps you really get at the meaning of a poem. It causes you to focus on the language and music of a poem, too.

Words/Lines	My Thoughts

Name: _____ Date: _____

Word Links

DIRECTIONS:

1. Read the poem aloud and to yourself several times.

2. As you reread, circle two important words in each line. Choose words that describe actions, create mood, or name a person, place, or thing.

3. Choose two words from Step 2.

4. Drawing on your past experiences with the words and how they work in the poem, write the emotions these words bring up in you in the Connotation column.

5. Then look the words up in a dictionary and write their main definitions in the Denotation column.

6. After completing the chart, reread the poem.

How This Helps

Thinking about the connotation of a word can help you understand and enjoy a part of a poem that you might have found confusing.

Word	Connotation	Denotation

50 Reproducible Strategy Sheets That Build Comprehension During Independent Reading   Scholastic Professional Books

Name: _____ Date: _____

Say It Your Way

Scholastic Professional Books

DIRECTIONS:

1. Read the poem out loud and to yourself several times.

2. As you reread, circle or highlight lines you found surprising or ones that you did not understand.

3. Write the lines down in the chart below.

4. Then write what you think the lines are saying in your own words.

5. Reread the poem. How did your paraphrasing help you understand the poem? Write your response on the back of this sheet.

Lines	My Paraphrase	What I Think It Means

Name: _____   Date: _____

Savor Your Senses

DIRECTIONS:

1. Read the poem out loud and to yourself several times.
2. As you reread, circle or highlight words that appeal to your sight, hearing, smell, touch, or taste. Note: Every sense might not be in each poem.
3. Write the words in the "Sense" boxes below.
4. Sketch the images that pop into your head when you read those words; use the back if you need more space.

How This Helps

Sensory words make descriptions in poems come alive. Being aware of sensory words helps you picture the poem in your mind and make connections to your own experiences.

Title: _____

Author _____

Sense	My Images
Sight Words	
Hearing Words	
Smell Words	
Taste Words	
Touch Words	

Helping Students Understand Literary Elements

Exploring Fiction

There are two main reasons for developing your students' grasp of different literary genres. First, understanding a genre allows students to use their knowledge about that genre's text structure to understand how new texts work. Second, understanding genre facilitates a reading and writing connection. When students understand how a genre works, they can begin to write in that genre, incorporating its structure and elements. Make sure students understand that a genre is a category, or kind, of literature with specific elements or traits. Give them examples of different genres like fantasy, fairy tales, or biography. The strategies in Part IV deepen students' comprehension of fiction, folk and fairy tales, biography/autobiography, informational books, and poetry.

Realistic Fiction, Historical Fiction, and Fantasy

The reproducibles in this first section can be used interchangeably with realistic fiction, historical fiction, and fantasy.

Who Is It?: Character Mapping

Getting to know the different characters in stories and books is part of what makes reading fun. Encourage students to pay attention to details about a character's physical appearance, personality, speech, thoughts, feelings, actions, and interactions with other characters. A character map helps students keep track of important facts and details about a character and makes drawing conclusions about a character easier. Students can use this graphic organizer during and after reading. It's also a helpful brainstorming and pre-writing tool when the students begin to write character sketches.

Climb the Mountain: Examine Plot Structure

The plot is the series of events that make up a story; it is what happens. During several read alouds, model for students how you identify the five parts of a plot: setting and characters, rising action, climax, falling action (denouement), and outcome. Keeping track of the plot helps students monitor the sequence of events and understand how the events fit together.

Model It

Helping Students Explore Plot

After reading a picture book or class novel, draw a plot outline on chart paper and share with them how you think about a story and identify the parts of the plot. Here's a plot outline I present with *Sadako and the Thousand Paper Cranes*:

Setting: Hiroshima, Japan
Characters: Sadako, Mother, Masahiro, Eiji, Kenji

Rising Action:
1. Sadako and her family go to Peace Park for a celebration.
2. Sadako feels dizzy when she runs and has to go into the hospital.
3. Sadako gets sicker, but folds paper cranes for good luck.
4. Sadako's friend Kenji dies, and Sadako thinks about death.

Climax: Sadako dies.

Outcome: Sadako's classmates finish folding the thousand paper cranes that are buried with her.

What's the Problem?: Identify Problem and Outcome

Stories are built around problems. Part of the excitement of reading comes from the desire to know how characters resolve the problems they encounter. Encourage your students to focus on the actions that lead to the problem's resolution. This skill—finding connections between actions and outcomes—will help students make deeper connections between events in the text and focus students on the main events of a story.

The Big Picture: Explore Genre: Realistic Fiction

The strategy for exploring realistic fiction helps students collect all of the key information about a story, novel, or play. Explain to students that when they finish reading something, there may be a lot of information that they need to keep straight. Using this strategy encourages students to organize their ideas and consider the entire story. Students can use it during reading to take notes or after reading to assess their comprehension.

Step Back in Time: Explore Genre: Historical Fiction

A historical fiction organizer focuses students on the unique characteristics of this genre, which includes details about a past time period—the daily and family life, the period-specific problems, and important events of that time. Discuss with students that historical fiction is fiction that takes place during the past and that often the author includes real details about that past time. If you have time in your study of historical fiction, you can start an interesting discussion in your class about how an author gets information for writing historical fiction, as well as the differences between primary and secondary sources. This discussion is an excellent opportunity to introduce students to methods of doing their own research.

IDEA BOX

A good activity to reinforce the meaning of genre is to have students divide a crate of books up according to genre. Ask them to give reasons for their choices.

Imaginary Worlds: Explore Genre: Fantasy

Use this strategy to help students recognize the characteristics associated with fantasy writing. Students need to know that most fantasy stories combine realistic features with fantastic qualities. Usually the stories deal with magic and the struggle between good and evil. Characters in fantasies are often faced with a quest, which is an adventure or a journey that a character must embark on to learn important information about himself or herself and the world. It is through the quest that the character learns an important lesson, and that lesson is usually connected to the theme of the book. Symbols are another very important element of fantasy writing. Model for students how symbols work in stories. And refer students to the explanations for the words quest and symbol that appear on their worksheet.

Think Aloud

Helping Students Understand Symbols

"When I look at the eagle on the top of the flagpole, I know it is a bird, but it is also more than a bird. It is what we call a *symbol*. A symbol is something that stands for something else. In the United States, an eagle stands for freedom—eagles are strong, independent birds and freedom is a strong and independent idea. We find eagles on the top of our flagpoles and on our money. Sometimes in stories, animals or things stand for other things. If the thing is important to the plot or important to a character, it might be a symbol, and I should take some time to think about what it might stand for."

Name: _____ Date: _____

Who Is It?
A Character Web

DIRECTIONS:

1. Preview the story or book and think about the main character. Write your predictions about the main character below.

2. Read the story or book.

3. As you read, jot down notes about the character on the character web.

4. After you read, ask yourself: "Did the character learn anything? Did the character change?" Write your answers on the back of this page, using the web to help you.

Make a Prediction

Preview the book and think about what the main character may be like. Write your predictions and ideas here.

_____

_____

_____

_____

_____

_____

_____

_____

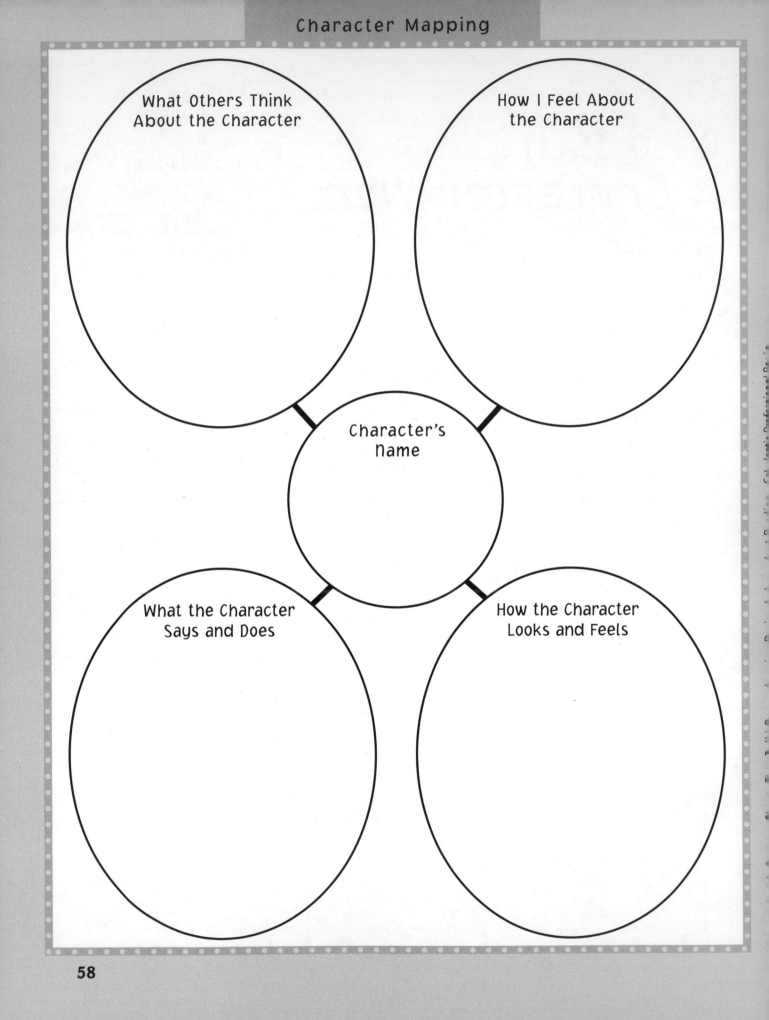

Name: _____   Date: _____

Climb the Mountain

DIRECTIONS:

1. Preview the story or book and set a purpose for reading.

2. As you read, underline words that clue you into time changes such as *next, later,* or *then*.

3. After reading, identify the five main parts of the story's plot (setting and characters, rising action, climax, falling action, outcome).

How This Helps

A Plot diagram helps you see how a story is put together. It clarifies how one action leads to another.

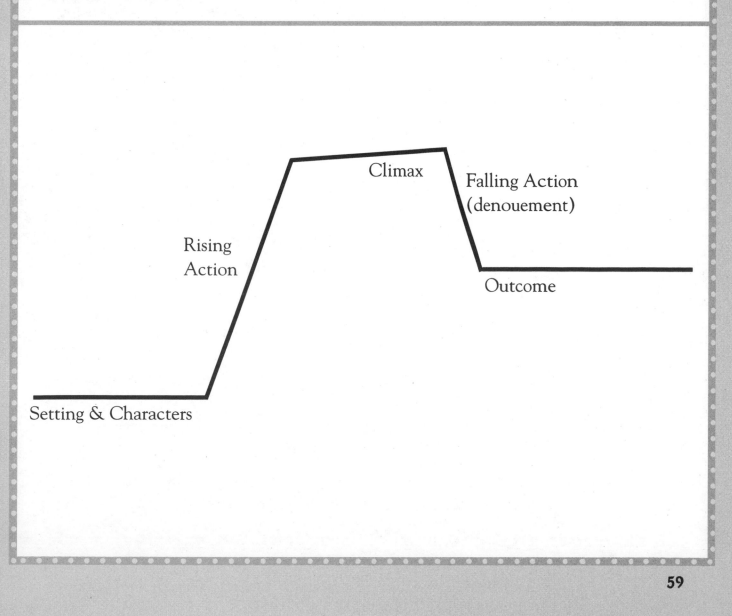

Climax

Falling Action (denouement)

Rising Action

Outcome

Setting & Characters

Name: _____   Date: _____

What's the Problem?

DIRECTIONS:

1. Preview the story or book and think about what problems might happen.
2. As you read, underline or highlight any problems that occur.
3. After you read, identify two main problems the main character faced and the actions the character took to solve each problem.

Main Character: _____

Problem One:	Problem Two:
Actions to Solve the Problem	Actions to Solve the Problem
Was It Solved?	Was It Solved?
How? or Why Not?	How? or Why Not?

Go the Extra Step

In what other ways could the problem have been solved? How would the story change? Write your thoughts on the back.

50 Reproducible Strategy Sheets That Build Comprehension During Independent Reading   Scholastic Professional Books

Name: _____ Date: _____

The Big Picture

DIRECTIONS:

1. Preview the story or book and think about how it will be realistic.

2. As you read, think about the details that make this story like real life.

3. After you read, fill in the organizer below.

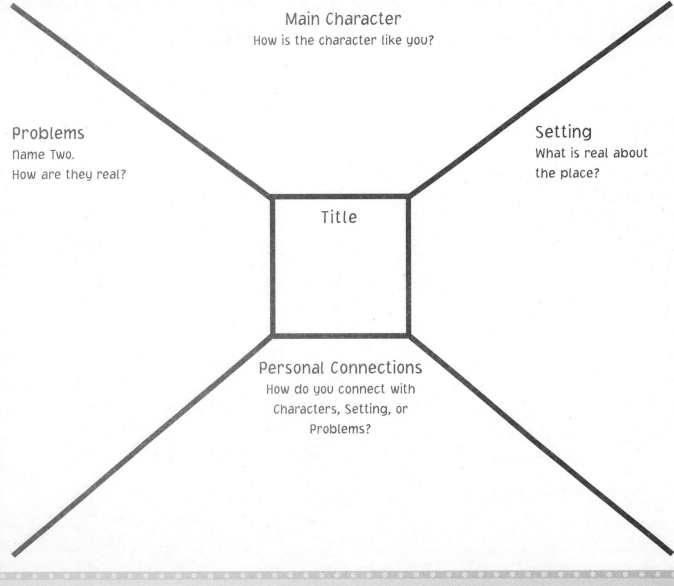

Main Character
How is the character like you?

Problems
Name Two.
How are they real?

Setting
What is real about the place?

Title

Personal Connections
How do you connect with Characters, Setting, or Problems?

Name: _____ Date: _____

Step Back in Time

DIRECTIONS:

1. Preview the story or book. On the back of this sheet write down what you know about the time period in which the story is set.

2. As you read, keep track of the historical details you learn.

3. After you read, ask yourself the questions listed below.

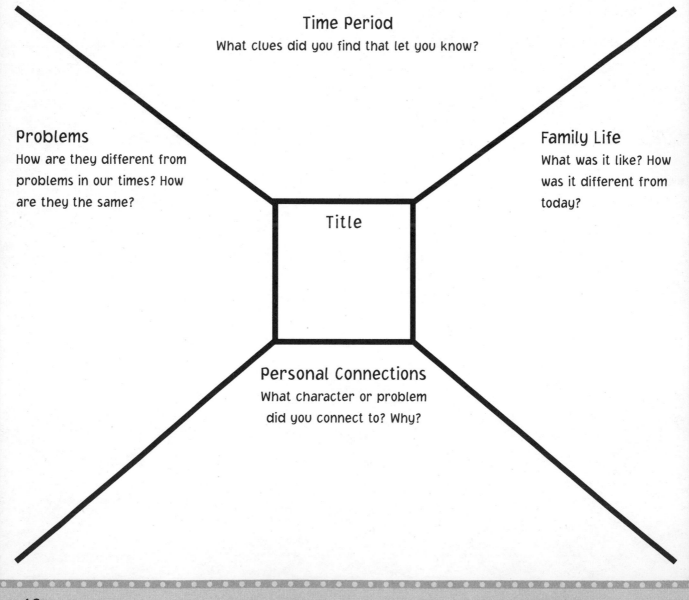

Time Period
What clues did you find that let you know?

Problems
How are they different from problems in our times? How are they the same?

Title

Family Life
What was it like? How was it different from today?

Personal Connections
What character or problem did you connect to? Why?

Name: _____   Date: _____

Imaginary Worlds

DIRECTIONS:

1. With a partner, read the characteristics of fantasy listed in the boxes below.

2. Read the story or book, thinking about the imaginary world and the details in the story that make it a fantasy.

3. After you read, answer the questions below.

How This Helps

This organizer helps you keep track of the important qualities that make the story or book a fantasy.

Fantasy Characteristics

Quest: A quest is an adventure or a journey that a character must embark on to learn important information about himself or herself and the world.

Symbol: A symbol is something that stands for something else. For example, an eagle stands for freedom, a dove for peace.

Good vs. Evil: In fantasy stories, good must usually face evil. Look out for goodness described as light and evil as shadow.

---

1. Title: _____

2. Describe the **quest**. _____

_____

_____

_____

_____

_____

_____

3. Setting: Describe imaginary word. _____

_____

_____

4. **Good vs. Evil:** List the forces of good and evil. _____

_____

_____

How does one overcome the other? _____

_____

_____

Go the Extra Step

Symbols: Did you notice anything in the story that works as a symbol (something that stands for something else)? _____

_____

_____

_____

What does the symbol add to the story? _____

_____

_____

Exploring Folk and Fairy Tales

The following strategy sheets can be used with folk and fairy tales. This genre of literature grew out of the oral storytelling tradition, which started thousands of years ago. Many of these tales deal with issues and problems that all children face and can relate to, no matter where they are from or when they live.

Tasks That Test: Explore Genre: Folk and Fairy Tales

In folk tales and fairy tales, a *task* is an undertaking or mission that one of the main characters must complete. Discuss with your students that tasks are a defining characteristic of folk and fairy tales, and often these tasks occur in threes and must be completed before some problem can be solved. Use this strategy to help your students identify the tasks in a tale and understand how the tasks affect the story. Students can also use this organizer as a springboard into writing their own tales: They can write another tale that uses the same task or brainstorm a new task their character must face.

What Makes It a Tale?: Explore Genre: Folk and Fairy Tales

By understanding the elements of the genre, students will ultimately be able to synthesize or pull together the different parts of the story. In my classroom, I introduce this genre by reading aloud folk tales and fairy tales and describing their characteristics. I think aloud to model for my students how I locate each element (see the example below). Then, I invite them to complete the strategy sheet as they read tales of their own choosing.

Think Aloud

Helping Students Understand Genre

"'Cinderella' has many important elements of a fairy tale. There is a definite evil force—Cinderella's wicked stepmother, who is always trying to stop Cinderella from being happy. There are also supernatural elements. Supernatural elements are things that are not of this earth—like fairies and elves. In Cinderella, the fairy godmother is a supernatural force. These elements help me figure out what is important in the story and point me to the moral or theme. Cinderella learns that no matter how bad a situation may seem, with a little help and patience, a person can change his or her destiny."

Name: _____   Date: _____

Tasks That Test

DIRECTIONS:

1. As you read, highlight the tasks the hero or heroine must complete.

2. After you read, think about and then answer the questions below.

Title: _____

Name the hero or heroine.	List the tasks the character faces.
What problem forces the hero/heroine to perform the tasks?	What does the character learn?
How does the task change the hero/ heroine?	How would you have faced the tasks in this story?

Name: _____   Date: _____

What Makes It a Tale?

DIRECTIONS:

1. Review the definitions of the elements of folk and fairy tales.

2. Read the story or book.

3. As you read, take notes on the forces of evil, magic numbers, and any supernatural elements.

4. After you read, think about the moral or lesson this tale teaches.

How This Helps

This organizer helps you keep track of the important elements in folk tales and fairy tales.

Elements of Folk and Fairy Tales

Forces of Evil: In many folk and fairy tales, an evil force works against the hero or heroine to try to stop them from being happy. (Example: The wicked stepmother in Snow White.)

Magic Numbers: In many folk and fairy tales, the numbers three and seven occur. (Think of the three pigs, the three bears, and the seven dwarfs.)

Supernatural Elements: Often in a folk or fairy tale, supernatural elements—things not of our earth—like fairies or elves come to the aid of the hero or heroine. (Example: Cinderella's fairy godmother)

1. **Forces of Evil:** What evil works against the hero/heroine?

_____

_____

_____

_____

_____

2. **Magic Numbers:** What numbers are important in this tale? Why?

_____

_____

_____

3. **Supernatural Elements:** List the supernatural elements in this tale. How do they help? _____

_____

_____

_____

How do they cause trouble? _____

_____

_____

Go the Extra Step

What lesson or moral does this tale teach?

_____

_____

_____

_____

_____

_____

Exploring Poetry

Reading and understanding poetry is a true joy. Poets love words and work hard to create vivid images and mesmerizing rhythms. Poems read aloud often enthrall children, who create pictures in their minds and get into the beat. In my experience, both inner city and suburban students, and even children who are hesitant to read anything, dive into poems eagerly. Reading aloud these short pieces full of images and music, rhythm and rhyme is an excellent way to hook students on poetry. Poems appeal to the senses and draw the reader into the poet's world immediately.

In school, students are often asked to decide what a poem "means." Instead, encourage students to focus first on the images, or pictures, that come into their minds as they read or listen to poetry. Introduce them to the tools poets use to create those pictures and invite them to try out the techniques in their own writing. After students fall in love with the words, you can begin talking about meaning

The strategies in this section encourage your students to reread, listen to sounds, and create images. Each sheet focuses on one element of the craft of poetry.

Dig Those Natural Rhythms: Explore Rhythm

Free verse poems have no regular rhyme scheme or meter, which may surprise students who associate poetry with rhymes. Read many free verse poems aloud to your students and then ask them what they think poetry is. Display a free verse poem on an overhead or on chart paper and ask your students, "What makes this a poem?" guiding them to notice word choice and rhythm.

This strategy sheet helps students focus on the strong, vivid language of poetry. You can also use it to make the reading and writing connection. Before writing free verse poems, students can brainstorm specific nouns and verbs that create images in their heads.

Give It a Break!: Identify Stanzas

A stanza is a group of lines in a poem set off by blank lines. Explain to students that a stanza in a poem is something like a paragraph in a story. A stanza usually develops one idea. It gives the poem a shape on the page and helps create meaning. Introduce the terms *couplet* and *quatrain* to your students. A *couplet* is a stanza made up of two lines. Usually, the end words rhyme. A *quatrain* is a stanza made up of four lines.

Rock and Rhyme: Determine Rhyme

Rhyme is often what first attracts students to poems. It adds music to poetry and makes a poem very pleasing to say aloud and to hear. Rhyme also makes it easier to memorize poems and can lead to interesting and surprising word choices. Introduce your students to end rhyme, which is the repetition of similar sounds that come at the end of lines of poetry. A fun activity to tune students' ears to end rhyme is to read a poem aloud and stop before the final word of the line. Students will jump right in with suggestions for completing the end rhyme.

Seeing With Simile: Find Similes

A simile is a comparison between two unlike things using the words *like* or *as*. Similes can help readers see an idea in a new way or make new connections. Use this strategy sheet to help students locate and think about similes in poems. It is also a good tool to use in connection to writing workshop. Students can use the similes they create or decipher as inspirations for their own poetry.

Think Aloud

Helping Students Understand Simile

"When I hear the line, *The tree was tall*, I don't get a very clear picture in my head. My idea of 'tall' might be very different from yours. So, I am going to try to think of a few other things that have something in common with a tall tree — like a giraffe's neck, a church steeple, a lighthouse on a cliff. After I come up with some things I can compare to the tallness of the tree, I can rewrite my sentence: '*The lonely tree stood tall as a lighthouse on a foggy cliff*'. Now, I ask my students, 'How did the simile improve the image of the tree?' and 'Can you think of other similes that might work?'"

Memorable Metaphors: Find Metaphors

A metaphor is a direct comparison between two unlike things that helps readers see something in a new way. Impress upon your students that a metaphor does not just say that one thing is like something else; it says it *is* something else. Metaphors are more difficult for students to spot because they do not use the comparison words *like* or *as*. Involve your students in reading metaphors by asking them questions such as:

◎ Why do you like this metaphor?

◎ Can you think of any other metaphors for this image?

◎ How is using a metaphor here different from using a simile?

Smooth Sounds: Use Alliteration

Alliteration is the repetition of the same consonant sound at the beginning of several words of a line of poetry. Your students will probably be most familiar with the use of alliteration in tongue twisters, which are often a good place to introduce this literary element. Poets use alliteration to create music and mood. Tongue twisters often create a silly or funny mood by using so many repeated sounds. Poets' use of alliteration is, naturally, more sparing.

Oh! The Sounds You'll Hear!: Identify Onomatopoeia

Onomatopoeia is the use of words that sound like the noises they describe. Poets often use onomatopoeia to add fun or emphasis to the words they use. Sounds help create images by appealing to the senses. Sounds can bring readers to a certain place and reinforce the meaning of the words.

IDEA BOX

Onomatopoeia

1. Present students with a sentence like *The wind blew.*
2. Brainstorm with students words that describe the wind blowing: *whoosh, whee, rattle, screech, clank*
3. Then rewrite the sentence using onomatopoeia: *"Whee!" sang the wind whistling down the sidewalk.*

Here are some more onomatopoetic words to share or brainstorm with your class: *splish, splosh, zing, ping, poof, thud, crash, bam, splat, pop, pow, whack, eek, click, tick tock, smack, wham, blam, rattle, zip, screech, plunk.*

Name: _____   Date: _____

Dig Those Natural Rhythms

DIRECTIONS:

1. Read the poem aloud and to yourself several times.

2. As you read, circle words that seem important or are repeated.

3. Choose two words and write them in the boxes.

4. Sketch the images that pop into your head when you read those words.

5. Set a purpose for rereading and read the poem again. Think about the ideas the poem emphasizes.

How This Helps

Free verse poems create strong images in your mind. Reading free verse focuses you on the beauty of the everyday rhythms of language.

Poem: _____   Poet: _____

Words _____

Words _____

Set a Purpose for Reading

Review the chart you created above and write about the ideas this poem is emphasizing (use the back of this sheet). Then reread with those ideas in mind.

Name: _____ Date: _____

Give It a Break!

DIRECTIONS:

1. Read the poem out loud and to yourself several times.

2. As you read, notice how the poem looks on the page and how the lines are organized.

3. Describe the organization in your answers below.

4. Reread the poem, and think about how the organization effects its meaning. Write your ideas on the back of this sheet.

How This Helps

Understanding how a poem is organized lets you focus on important ideas in the poem.

Poem: _____

Poet: _____

How many stanzas are there? _____

How many lines are in each stanza? _____

List repeated sounds or phrases. Is there a pattern? _____

_____

_____

List words that rhyme or create music in the poem. _____

_____

_____

Listen for a rhythm. What words are stressed? _____

_____

_____

Name: _____ Date: _____

Rock and Rhyme

DIRECTIONS:

1. Read the poem out loud and to yourself several times.
2. As you read, listen to the sounds of words as you say them. Ask yourself what effect the music is creating.
3. Describe the sounds, the rhymes, and the repetitions in the chart below.
4. Set a purpose for rereading, then read the poem again. Think about how the rhyme adds to its meaning.

How This Helps

Understanding rhyme shows you how the sound works to add to the poem's meaning. It also adds enjoyment to reading by pleasing your ears.

Listen to the Rhythm

Oral Reading: Oral reading is reading out loud. It helps you key in on the repeated sounds, rhymes, and repetitions.

Choral Reading: Choral reading is reading aloud with a group of people. You might notice that reading aloud together gives you a better feel for the rhythm of a poem. Sometimes the sounds make more noise when you hear others reading aloud.

Poem: _____ Poet: _____

Words	Effects the Music of the Words Create

Reproducible Graphic Organizer Sheets That Build Comprehension During Independent Reading   Scholastic Professional Books

Name: _____ Date: _____

Seeing With Simile

DIRECTIONS:

1. Read the poem out loud and to yourself several times.
2. As you read, underline or highlight any similes that you find; look for the key words *like* and *as* that can signal similes.
3. Explain the similes below.
4. Reread the poem and think about how the similes add to pictures you get in your mind. Write your thoughts on the back of this sheet.

How This Helps

Understanding similes helps you see things in new ways and make connections between things that seem different at first.

About Simile

A *simile* is a comparison between two unlike things using the words *like* or *as*. For example, "The willow's music is like a soprano/ Delicate and thin." (From *Simile: Willow and Ginkgo* by Eve Merriam.) The willow's music is compared to a soprano's voice. The thing common to both: their music is "delicate and thin" and beautiful to hear.

Poem: _____ Poet: _____

Simile: _____

What two things are being compared? _____

_____

How are they alike? _____

_____

What other comparisons could you make? _____

_____

Name: _____ Date: _____

Memorable Metaphors

DIRECTIONS:

1. Read the poem out loud and to yourself several times. Highlight any metaphors you find.
2. Choose a metaphor and describe it below.
3. Reread the poem and think about how the metaphors add to your understanding of it. Write your thoughts on the back of this sheet.

How This Helps

Understanding metaphors helps you see things in new ways and make connections between things that seem different at first.

About Metaphor

A *metaphor* is a direct comparison between two unlike things.

For example: "Morning is/ a new sheet of paper/ for you to write on."

(From "Metaphor," *A Sky Full of Poems* by Eve Merriam). The morning is being compared to a new sheet of paper. Both things are new, fresh, and clean. Both morning and a blank sheet of paper can be turned into something new.

Poem: _____ Poet: _____

Metaphor _____

What two things are being compared? _____

_____

How are they alike? _____

_____

What other comparisons could you make? _____

_____

_____

Name: _____ Date: _____

Smooth Sounds

DIRECTIONS:

1. Read the poem out loud and to yourself several times.

2. As you read, underline or highlight any repeated consonant sounds.

3. Ask yourself what effect the repetition is creating.

4. Set a purpose for rereading and read the poem again. Think about how the alliteration adds to your understanding and enjoyment of the poem.

How This Helps

Hearing alliteration in a poem helps you enjoy the music of a poem and focuses you on words that may be important to the poem's meaning.

About Alliteration

Alliteration is the repetition of the same consonant sound at the beginning of two or more words in a line of poetry. For example: *She sells seashells by the seashore.* Both the *s* and the *sh* sounds are repeated. They make a hissing sound like the sound of the waves when you hold a shell up to your ear.

Poem: _____ Poet: _____

What words are alliterative? _____

What sound is repeated? _____

How is the sound important in the poem? _____

_____

Set a Purpose

Review the alliteration you noted in the chart above and think about the alliteration. Why do you think the poet chose to repeat this sound? Write your response on the back of this sheet.

Name: _____ Date: _____

Oh! The Sounds You'll Hear!

DIRECTIONS:

1. Read the poem out loud and to yourself several times.

2. As you read, underline or highlight any onomatopoetic sounds.

3. Ask yourself what effect the onomatopoeia is creating.

4. Reread the poem and think about how the onomatopoeia adds to your understanding and enjoyment of the poem.

How This Helps

Hearing onomatopoeia in a poem helps you picture images through sounds in your mind and focus on words that may be important to the poem's meaning.

About Onomatopoeia

Onomatopoeia is the use of words that sound like the noises they describe. For example: "The rusty spigot/ sputters/ utters/ a splutter/ splatters a smattering of drops." (From *It Doesn't Always Have to Rhyme* by Eve Merriam.) The words *sputter*, and *splatter* make a *smattering* sound, like what they mean.

Poem: _____ Poet: _____

What words are onomatopoetic? _____

_____

_____

How do they help you imagine the scene? _____

_____

_____

Draw what you see in your mind. Use the back of this page.

Exploring Biography and Autobiography

Begin your study of biography and autobiography by guiding your class through a KWL chart. Make sure students know that a biography is the story of a person's life, written by another person, while an autobiography is the story of a person's life, written by that person. Curiosity and the desire to learn about a famous or influential person attract students to biographies and autobiographies. Use the reproducibles in this section to focus your students on the important elements of both genres.

Making a Difference: Note Key Accomplishments

This strategy will help your students identify the key accomplishments in a person's life. The worksheet asks the students to describe these accomplishments in chronological order and give examples from the text. Students can use the worksheet as an organizer for writing a summary of a person's life.

Life's Building Blocks: Determine Important Influences

People's lives are filled with influences from the places they've lived, the people they've met, and events they've lived through. Explain that these outside forces shape and change people's lives. Review Cause and Effect with students (a cause is a first action or event that results in an effect; see pages 39–40, 44).

How Am I Like You?: Make Connections

Introduce this strategy by explaining to students that their job as readers of biography and autobiography is to figure out how they feel about the person whose life story they are reading. To do this, encourage them to begin connecting to the subject as they read by jotting down notes in their journal or on sticky notes, commenting on and reacting to the person's life.

How They Helped the World: Synthesize Information

An excellent reading strategy that works well with biography and autobiography is synthesizing. Synthesizing is a critical thinking skill that helps students put together parts to form a whole. Students can use this worksheet to gather up details about key topics and figure out how they fit together. Encourage your students to read closely and highlight key details in the person's life, jotting them down on sticky notes or in their journal.

Name: _____ Date: _____

Making a Difference

DIRECTIONS:

1. Preview the biography or autobiography and set a purpose for reading.

2. As you read, mark the important accomplishments in this person's life.

3. After you read, record what you have learned about the person in the chart below.

Set a Purpose

Preview and think about what you already know about this person's life. On the back of this sheet list two to three things you hope to learn.

Person's Name _____

Important Accomplishments	Evidence From the Story
Young Adulthood:	
Adulthood:	

Go the Extra Step

Reread your notes from the chart. Ask yourself, "Do I admire this person?"
Explain why or why not on the back of this sheet.

50 Reproducible Strategy Sheets That Build Comprehension During Independent Reading *Scholastic Professional Books*

Name: _____ Date: _____

Life's Building Blocks

DIRECTIONS:

1. Preview the biography or autobiography and make a prediction about this person's early experiences; write it on the back of this sheet, giving support for your prediction.

2. Now, read to discover what this person's life was like.

3. As you read, underline, highlight, or use sticky notes to mark the important settings, people, or events that shaped this person's life.

4. After reading, think about how these events (causes) affected the person (effects). Record what you have learned about the person in the chart below.

CAUSES: Life-Shaping Elements	EFFECTS: How did these events change the person's life?
Family:	
Other People:	
Events:	

Name: _____ Date: _____

How Am I Like You?

DIRECTIONS:

1. Preview the biography or autobiography and set a purpose for your reading.

2. Now, read to discover ways in which you may be like this person.

3. As you read, jot down predictions, notes, and comments about the person's life in the first column of the chart.

4. After reading, think about what the person was like and how you feel about him or her. Write about the connections you made—ways you are like him or her.

Set a Purpose
Preview the book or article and think about ways you are like this person. Write your ideas on the back of this sheet.

Predictions and Notes	Connections I Made
To setting or early years:	
To people:	
To what he/she did:	
To what he/she said:	

Name: _____ Date: _____

How They Helped the World

DIRECTIONS:

1. Preview the biography or autobiography and set a purpose for your reading.

2. Read and underline, highlight, or use sticky notes to keep track of key details about the person's family, school, work, major achievements, and personality.

3. Record what you have learned about the person in the chart below.

4. Finally, reread your notes and think about how this person helped the world. Write about his/her most important contribution on the back of this sheet.

Set a Purpose
Preview the book and think about why it was written about this person. Write your ideas on the back of this sheet.

Key Topics	What I learned from the reading:
School	
Work	
Achievements	
Personality	

Exploring Informational Books

Students will encounter nonfiction reading material in all subjects and, of course, on standardized tests. When students understand the structure of expository texts, they can more readily navigate through them and recall facts from magazines, newspapers, and informational picture and chapter books. The strategy sheets in this section will help students recognize nonfiction text structures. Remind students that previewing the text and making predictions are effective strategies for reading and understanding nonfiction as well as fiction.

Seeking Solutions: Identify Problem-Solution Text Structure

The problem-solution pattern is often used to organize nonfiction pieces. Discuss with students that sometimes a paragraph might pose a problem and a solution, and sometimes a whole article or book might be devoted to "solving" one problem. Understanding this pattern can help students sort out the problems or issues raised in nonfiction writing and identify the solutions provided in the text. Encourage students to think about the relationship between the problem and the outcomes. Extend this activity into critical thinking by having students offer alternate solutions to problems.

Do the Facts Add Up?: Distinguish Fact and Opinion

When reading informational books, students need to be aware of the difference between factual statements and opinions. A factual statement can be proven objectively. An opinion reflects a writer's subjective beliefs or feelings. Often the new information a writer presents explains factual issues and ideas

IDEA BOX

Gathering New Information

Informational texts often present students with new information and vocabulary. Explain to students that good readers keep track of new information they learn while they read. There are many different ways to do this: underlining, highlighting, taking notes in margins or on sticky notes to mark important parts, and using stars or question marks to identify confusing parts.

Sometimes I model placing sticky notes on pages during a read-aloud to show where I learned new information or discovered a new word.

with a slant (opinion). And sometimes a writer can make a point so strongly that readers change their ideas and opinions on a topic. Explain to students that it is important to be able to identify the facts and to understand both the author's viewpoint and the evidence he or she presents to support it.

Questioning the Reader: Ask Questions

Questioning is a great strategy to use before, during, and after reading. It keeps students wondering as they read and helps involve them in the text. It also helps them pinpoint what they understand and what parts confuse them. Students who are not familiar with this strategy can begin with self-questioning, such as "What am I reading about?" "What don't I understand?" and "Which parts should I reread?" When you read aloud to your class, model, by thinking aloud, the questions that come into your mind before, during, and after reading. When they see you taking time to wonder about information, they will grasp its importance.

Once Upon a Time . . . : Make Personal Connections

To deepen students' understanding and enjoyment of reading informational texts, encourage them to make personal connections to the topics and the new information they learn. This strategy asks students to connect to different aspects of an informational book, such as the ideas, new facts, photos, and charts. Before asking students to connect to this information, review with them how to read a chart, diagram, and graph.

IDEA BOX

Finding Opinions

After introducing fact and opinion, I do this activity with my class: I brainstorm with students a list of words that signal an opinion is coming, and list them on a chart. Here are some words my students came up with: *might, think, feel, maybe, could have been, should, must, believe, want, better, best, worst, most, least, prettiest, smartest.*

When we have a good list, I post the chart in the classroom for students to refer to and invite students to add new "opinion" words they find in their readings.

Name: _____ Date: _____

Seeking Solutions

DIRECTIONS:

1. As you read, underline, highlight, or use sticky notes to mark two problems or issues the author points out in the book, article, or textbook chapter you are reading.

2. After reading, go back and skim these sections to discover the possible solutions that have been offered.

3. Record what you have learned in the chart below.

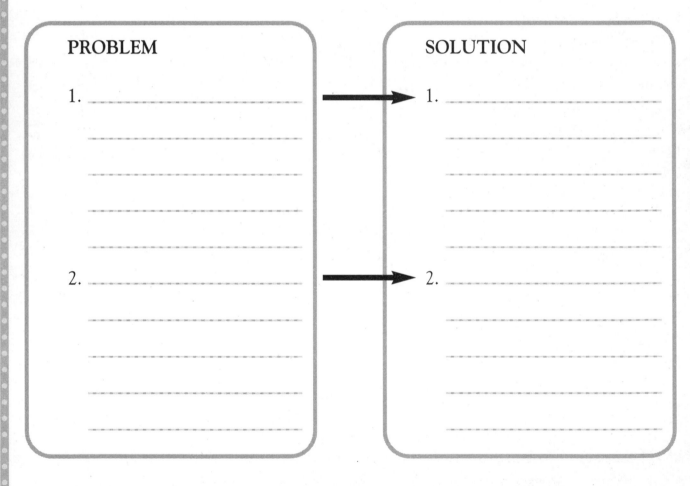

PROBLEM	SOLUTION
1.	1.
2.	2.

My Opinion: Reread your ideas in the chart above and on the back of this sheet, write which solution you feel is best. Offer at least two reasons for your choice.

50 Reproducible Strategy Sheets That Build Comprehension During Independent Reading · Scholastic Professional Books

Name: _____ Date: _____

Do the Facts Add Up?

DIRECTIONS:

1. As you read, use sticky notes to mark the facts the author uses.

2. After reading, record four important facts below.

3. List two of the author's opinions below.

4. Reread your notes. Do you think the facts support the author's opinion? Why or why not? Write your answer on the back of this sheet.

Set a Purpose

Preview the book and think about what you already know or feel about this topic. Write your ideas here. _____

_____

Four New Facts

1. _____

2. _____

3. _____

4. _____

List Two of the Author's Opinions. (Look for phrases that tell you an opinion is coming: *might, maybe, possibly, could have happened.*)

1. _____

2. _____

Name: _____ Date: _____

Questioning The Reader

DIRECTIONS:

1. Preview the text. On the back of this page, fast write about what you already know about the topic.

2. As you read the text, use sticky notes to mark parts that are hard to understand. Use the "During Reading" section below to retell confusing parts and clarify them.

3. After reading, record your questions and answers in the chart below.

During Reading

As you read the article, ask yourself, "Is this information making sense?" Clarify by rereading then retelling any confusing parts. _____

_____

_____

_____

After Reading

When you finish the article or text, answer the questions below.
What did I learn? _____

_____

What questions do I still have? _____

_____

_____

Where could I look to find out more information? _____

Name: _____   Date: _____

Once Upon a Time . . .

DIRECTIONS:

1. Preview and set a purpose for reading; write it below.

2. Read the text. As you read, use sticky notes to mark information that you connect to.

3. Record the new information and your connections in the chart below.

4. On the back of this sheet, write about how your feelings or thoughts have changed.

Set a Purpose

Preview and think about what you already know about this topic. What other things would you like to find out? _____

_____

Part of Book/Text	What I Learned	Connections I Made
An Idea or Opinion		
New Information		
A Photo or Illustration		
A Map/Graph/Chart		

PART 5

Strategies to Help Students With Word Study

Understanding new words is a crucial aspect of reading comprehension, and it is especially important with nonfiction. While reading independently, students will encounter words that they do not know. The dictionary is a great tool, but it is not always the best choice when engrossed in an exciting book. When I am reading and I come across a word that I do not know, I rarely (if ever) stop reading, find a dictionary, and look up the word. Instead, I look for clues in diagrams, read on for definitions, descriptions, synonyms, antonyms, or other context clues. When reading independently, students need to develop these skills for tackling new words by themselves. The strategy sheets in this section will help you give students a framework for thinking about and analyzing new words in a text.

The purpose of the following vocabulary sheets is word study, and the aim of each activity has been set for the students. Understanding the purpose of their work before they begin will help students concentrate on what they are learning and why it is important.

Word Detectives: Use Context Clues

This strategy encourages young readers to build their reading vocabulary by becoming word detectives. Show students how thinking about context clues and information from illustrations or charts helps them become word sleuths. By recognizing that all readers encounter new words and showing students how we can use a variety of strategies to figure out their meaning, you help students avoid frustration when faced with new vocabulary. Here are some guidelines to help your students become word detectives:

- Have students write two to three new words on a sticky note that they found tough.

- Ask students to write the page number on which they found each word.

- Show students how you use context clues to figure out a word's meaning.

- Repeat your modeling and think aloud process many times.

Invite students to help you use context clues. Once students "get it," have them work in pairs to figure out their words' meanings.

Questioning the Word: Create a Vocabulary Web

Engaging in an active question-and-answer "dialogue" with new words teaches students the importance of wondering—to discover what they know and do not know. Once questioning guidelines have been established, students can set personal vocabulary goals. Introduce students to different levels of questioning— from direct to open-ended questions. Encourage students to use higher-level thinking skills by asking open-ended questions that have more than one answer.

Context to Connection: Perform a Word Study

When students can link what they already know to an unfamiliar term, they create a context that will help them remember the word more easily. Many students memorize words on vocabulary lists and never use them after their weekly vocabulary quiz. By creating a personal context for the new word encountered, students can integrate this new vocabulary into their speaking and writing.

Take Apart a Word: Perform a Word Study

Before employing this strategy, introduce students to various roots, prefixes, and suffixes. Model for students how you would deconstruct a word using this strategy, then have students work in pairs to support each other's learning. Tell your students that some words work like machines: words have different parts that work together to make them run, to make sense. Sometimes the word parts are even interchangeable. Once you understand how a part works in one word, you can carry over what you know to the next word that uses that same part.

Name: _____ Date: _____

Word Detectives

DIRECTIONS:

1. As you read a text, use sticky notes to mark new vocabulary words.
2. After reading, record the sentence/page that contains a new word in the chart below.
3. Use context clues to make a good guess of the word's meaning. Hint: Sometimes you have to read a few sentences before or after the word to get its meaning.
4. Look up the word in the dictionary to see if you made an accurate guess.
5. Then, think of other words the author could have used.

Purpose

Think about what you already know about this topic and any new words. Read to analyze a new vocabulary word.

New Word	New Word
Sentence With Word	Sentence With Word
My Guess	My Guess
Dictionary Definition	Dictionary Definition
Other Words	Other Words

Go the Extra Step

What clues helped you figure out the meaning of the words?

Name: _____ Date: _____

Questioning The Word

DIRECTIONS:

1. As you read, use sticky notes to mark new vocabulary words.

2. Record one new word in the web below.

3. Think about and answer the questions about the word in the chart.

4. Share your ideas with a reading partner.

Purpose

Think about what you already know about this topic and any new words. Read to analyze a new vocabulary word.

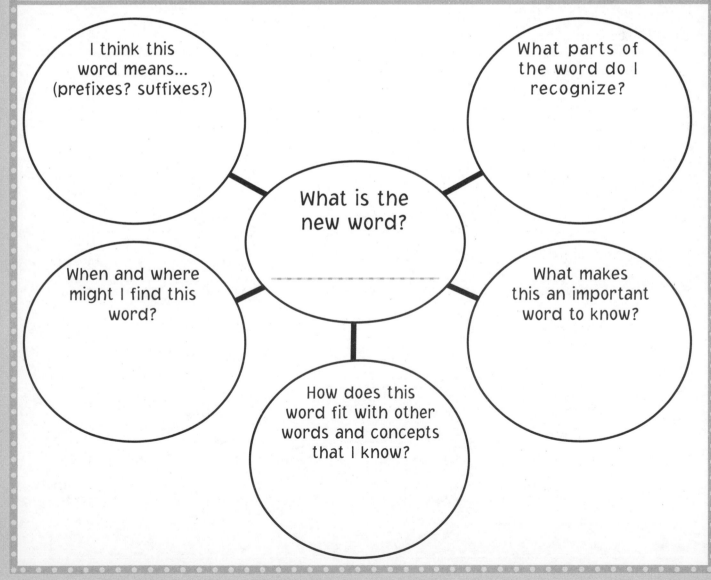

I think this word means... (prefixes? suffixes?)

What parts of the word do I recognize?

What is the new word?

_____

When and where might I find this word?

What makes this an important word to know?

How does this word fit with other words and concepts that I know?

Context to Connection

Name: _____   Date: _____

DIRECTIONS:

1. As you read, use sticky notes to mark new vocabulary words.
2. Record one new word below and provide the context in which it was used.
3. Think about and answer the questions about the word.
4. Share your personal connection with a reading partner and go the extra step by thinking about how connecting to this word adds to the text.

Purpose

Think about what you already know about this topic and any new words. Read to connect a new vocabulary word to your life.

1. Word _____

2. Word used in context _____

   _____

3. My definition using context clues _____

   _____

4. I'll probably encounter this word in (conversations, books, or TV shows about people, places, events, or situations): _____

   _____

5. I'll remember this word by connecting it to... _____

   _____

6. How does this words connect to or add to a character, setting, or event in the text? _____

   _____

50 Reproducible Strategy Sheets That Build Comprehension During Independent Reading · Scholastic Professional Books

Name: _____   Date: _____

Take Apart a Word

DIRECTIONS:

1. As you read, use sticky notes to mark new vocabulary words.

2. Record one new word that has prefixes and/or suffixes in the box below.

3. Think about and answer the questions about the word.

4. Share your personal connection with a reading partner and go the extra step by writing about how this word was important to the text.

Purpose

Test your knowledge of word parts and devise a definition based on that knowledge.

Word _____

Sentence the word is used in: _____

_____

Word parts I recognize (prefix, suffix, root): _____

_____

What the parts mean: _____

_____

Other words I know with this root or base: _____

_____

My definition based on my knowledge of the word parts: _____

_____

How is this word important to the text? What other words could the author have chosen? _____

_____

notes